Explorers

Written by
Hazel Songhurst

Devised by
Robin Wright

Illustrated by
Rachael O'Neill

DERRYDALE BOOKS

NEW YORK • AVENEL, NEW JERSEY

CONTENTS

Produced by Zigzag Publishing Ltd,
The Barn, Randolph's Farm,
Brighton Road, Hurstpierpoint,
West Sussex, BN6 9EL

Edited by Nicola Wright
Designed by Chris Leishman
Photographs by Tony Potter

Color separations by RCS Graphics Ltd, Leeds
Printed by Canale Italy

This edition published by Derrydale Books, distributed by
Outlet Book Company, Inc., a Random House Company,
40 Engelhard Avenue, Avenel, New Jersey 07001

Random House
New York • Toronto • London • Sydney • Auckland

ISBN 0-517-10223-4

10 9 8 7 6 5 4 3 2 1

ABOUT THIS BOOK

Explorers travel into unknown territory, through dense forests and jungles, across scorching, dry deserts or frozen polar wastelands. Some dive far beneath the sea and others are rocketed into outer space. Explorers are brave and love adventure.

This book has lots of fun ideas for playing explorers. It shows you, step-by-step, how to make a mosquito hat to wear in the jungle, a survival-kit carrier to take with you on any expedition, and ideas for simple shelters to build.

Bring the jungle into your own bedroom by making a giant picture on the wall, or be a wildlife explorer and collect specimens in a handmade bug jar. Make alien masks and your own astronaut helmet and oxygen pack for a space adventure.

There are exploring games, too. Play Arctic racing with your friends, or help explorers escape from a pyramid maze.

There are also fascinating facts about some famous real-life explorers. You can learn useful survival tips and distress signals and brush up on the terms explorers use on expeditions.

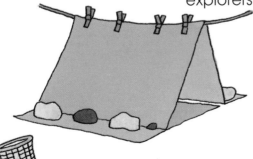

WHAT YOU NEED

On these pages you can see the things you need to play the games in the book, and to make your own kits for all kinds of expeditions.

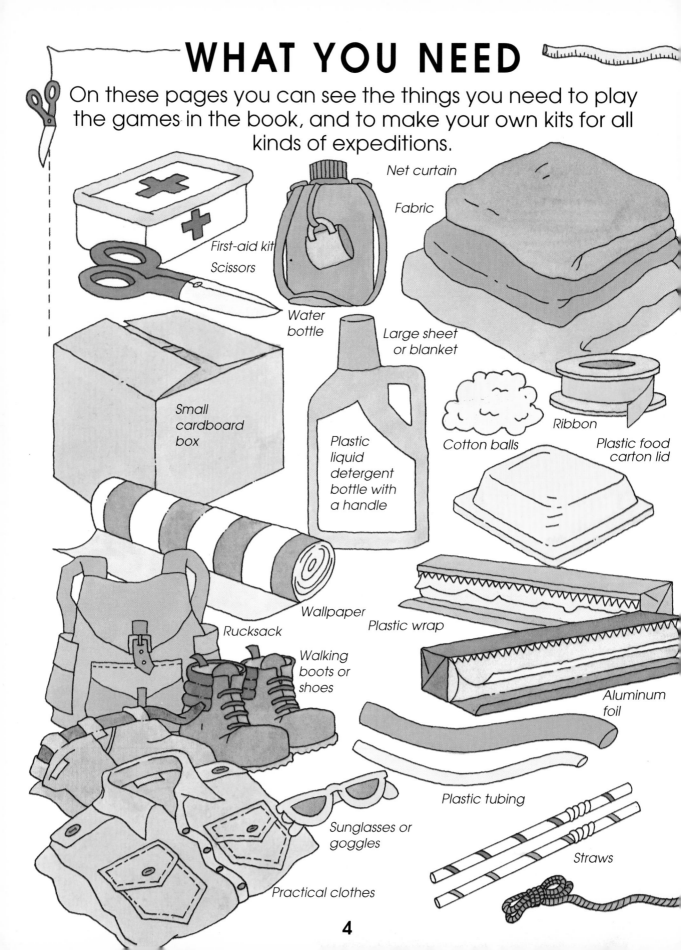

First-aid kit

Scissors

Water bottle

Net curtain

Fabric

Large sheet or blanket

Small cardboard box

Plastic liquid detergent bottle with a handle

Cotton balls

Ribbon

Plastic food carton lid

Wallpaper

Plastic wrap

Rucksack

Walking boots or shoes

Aluminum foil

Plastic tubing

Sunglasses or goggles

Straws

Practical clothes

Rations

Ruler

Paint brush

Pencil

Cellophane tape

Rubber bands

Felt-tip pens

Pen top

String

Craft knife

Plasticine

Small glass jar with a plastic lid

Poster-tack

Large glass jar

Paints

Plastic bottles

Fabric glue

Colored paper

Colored cardboard or posterboard

Glue

Using a craft knife

For safety, always tilt the cutting edge of the blade away from you and cut past your body. Place what you are cutting on a workboard, or a thick piece of cardboard.

Cut this way

Cardboard to protect table

REMEMBER!

Anything sharp or hot can harm you. When you see this danger sign, ask an adult to help you.

CLOTHES

Explorers wear comfortable, practical clothes that suit the climate and kind of terrain they are travelling in. Here are some ideas to help you make your own explorer outfits.

In a cold climate you need:

In a hot climate you need:

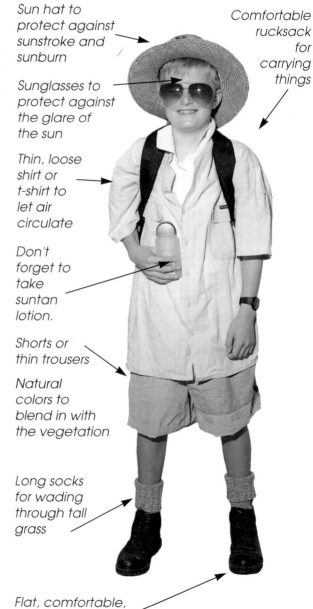

Woolly hat for warmth (one-third of your body's heat is lost through your head)

Goggles for protection against snowblindness

Scarf (to keep your neck warm but also because hot air rises and escapes around your neck)

Thick, waterproof jacket

Gloves

Bright or fluorescent colors to show up in bad weather conditions

Lots of layers of clothes to trap warm air between them

Thick socks and boots to keep out cold and wet

Sun hat to protect against sunstroke and sunburn

Sunglasses to protect against the glare of the sun

Thin, loose shirt or t-shirt to let air circulate

Don't forget to take suntan lotion.

Shorts or thin trousers

Natural colors to blend in with the vegetation

Long socks for wading through tall grass

Flat, comfortable, walking shoes or shoes.

Comfortable rucksack for carrying things

Anti-mosquito hat

Make this anti-mosquito hat for protection against flying pests in tropical climates.

You need:

Large piece of cardboard
Piece of thin net curtain
Piece of string
Fabric glue
Scissors
Cellophane tape

You could use the netting from fruit or vegetable bags instead of net curtain.

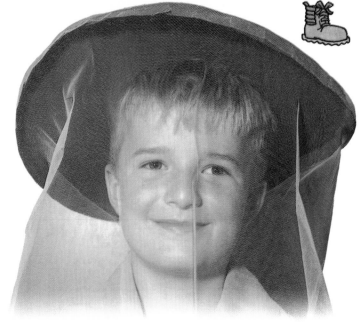

1 Draw around a large plate or tray onto the cardboard and cut the circle out. Cut $^3/_4$ in slits all around the edge.

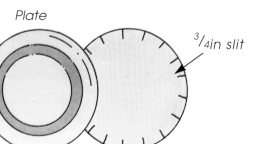

Plate

$^3/_4$in slit

2 Measure around your head with a piece of string and tie a knot. Tape the string to the cardboard and cut out the circle inside it.

Cut out a circle to fit your head.

You could attach the netting to an old hat with a brim.

3 Remove the string and place the ring on your head. Close the net curtain around to see how much you need.

The net curtain should reach down to your shoulders.

4 Bend down the slits on the brim and glue the net curtain to them.

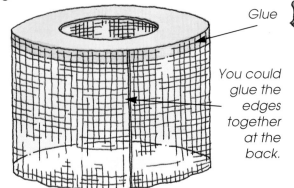

Glue

You could glue the edges together at the back.

SURVIVAL

People cannot survive without food and water.
Explorers must carry a supply of food and plenty
of water to keep healthy.

 Fresh food quickly goes off, so real explorers take dried, powdered and canned foods that give them a balanced diet of proteins, fats and carbohydrates.

Here are some suggestions for energy-giving rations that you could take with you:

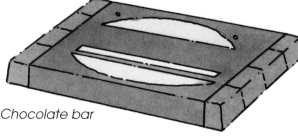

Nuts

Dried fruit

Fresh water in a clean, plastic bottle

Chocolate bar

Hard candy

 Water is very important. Without it, you would die in a few days. When real explorers run out of water they drink melted snow or ice, dew or rainwater.

Survival-kit carrier

Make this handy survival-kit carrier. Pack it with items you need for your expedition.

You need:

*Two pieces of thick fabric
 (12$^{1}/_{2}$in x 8$^{3}/_{4}$in, and 12$^{1}/_{2}$in x 4in)
Fabric glue
Tape or ribbon (17$^{3}/_{4}$in long)
Scissors
Ruler
Survival equipment, including first-aid
 items (band-aids, bandages, scissors,
 tweezers, insect-bite cream, snake-bite
 lotion), and string, compass, penknife etc.*

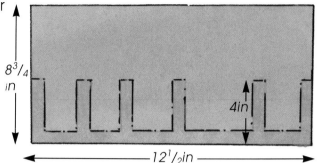

1 Spread fabric glue along the bottom and sides and in lines as shown. Make as many spaces as you need for all your items.

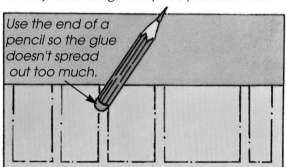

Use the end of a pencil so the glue doesn't spread out too much.

2 Glue on the smaller fabric strip (it looks good in a different color). Press down firmly along the lines with the end of a pencil. Leave to dry. Then store your equipment in the pockets.

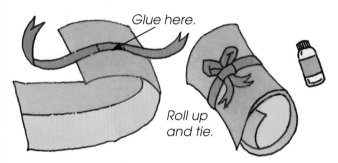

Glue here.

Roll up and tie.

3 Glue the middle of your tape or ribbon on the back of one edge. Roll up the kit from the other end. Wrap the tape or ribbon around the bundle and tie a bow so it can be quickly undone in an emergency.

Fill a small empty bottle with water and pretend it is "snake-bite" lotion!

FINDING THE WAY

Explorers need maps to guide them through unfamiliar territory, and to point out danger areas such as swampy ground, or obstacles such as high mountains.

The first people to explore a new territory make a map of the area giving a route for future travellers to follow.

Make this imaginary explorer's map and use it to play a game with your friends.

You need:

Large sheet of paper (19in x 14in)
Colored paper
Felt-tip pens
Scissors, poster-tack
Pencil, ruler

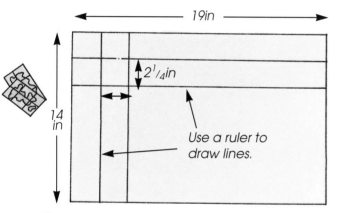

19in

14 in

2¹/₄in

Use a ruler to draw lines.

	A	B	C	D	E	F	G	H
1								
2								
3								
4								
5								
6								

1 Make a pencil mark every 6cm along all four sides of the sheet of paper. Join each mark with the one opposite to divide the paper into squares.

2 Number the squares down the left-hand side 1 to 6. Write the letters A to H in the squares across the top.

Map features

Trace two of each of the features on page 11 onto colored paper. Cut them out and stick poster-tack on the back. Each feature is worth the number of points shown.

Feature	Score	Feature	Score
Tarantula spider	Minus 10	Gold mine	10
Tiger	Minus 9	Drinking hole	9
Gorilla	Minus 8	Snake-bite lotion	8
Swamp	Minus 7	Chimpanzee	
Snake pit	Minus 6	(to guide you)	7
Unfriendly		Rope ladder	6
native camp	Minus 5	Elephant (to carry you)	5
Shark pool	Minus 4	Food	4
Crocodile	Minus 3	Lost city	3
Thorn tree	Minus 2	Truck	2
Mosquitoes	Minus 1	Friendly native camp	1

How to play

One player takes the map and, without the other players seeing, sticks each feature in a square, using the blob of poster-tack. The blank squares which are left are not worth any points.

Each of the other players then takes turns naming a square on the map, for example, C5. If C5 has an elephant on it, the player scores 5 points. If a player picks a square with a crocodile on it, he or she loses 3 points. After everyone has had five turns, add up the scores to find the winner. (Use a calculator if you get confused!) Then it is someone else's turn to put the features on the map.

   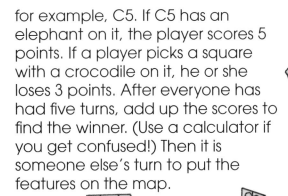

PITCHING CAMP

After a day's travelling, explorers look for a place to camp. For a comfortable night's rest, they must choose the site carefully.

These are some of the things that real explorers look for.

Warm spot (not in a hollow or valley where cold air collects and causes frost)

Trees for a supply of wood

Nearby water supply

Dry, flat ground

 Shelter from the wind (Do not point the opening of a tent into the wind. Point it east, so it faces the sun in the morning.).

Shelters

Some explorers do not carry tents. Instead, they use natural materials such as sticks, leaves and rocks, and even snow, to build shelters.

Snow shelter. The hard, frozen walls stop the heat from bodies escaping.

Rock shelter - rocks piled up on the sides of a hollow with a roof made from sticks, grass and moss

Stick dome - like a teepee with long sticks in a circle, tied together at the top, then sticks and moss woven in between

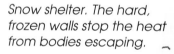

Make your own shelter

Here are some easy shelters to make, or make up your own.

This is a good shelter indoors or out.

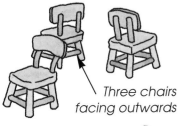

Three chairs facing outwards

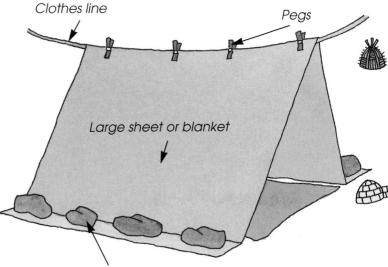

Clothes line

Pegs

Large sheet or blanket

Heavy bricks, stones or other objects

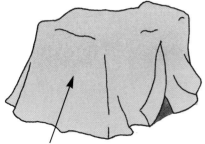

Large sheet or blanket draped over

Ask an adult to help you make this teepee.

Six very tall garden canes tied around with string at one end. Spread the other ends out in a circle and push them into the ground.

Large sheet or blanket wrapped around

In dry, warm weather, you might be able to spend the night in your shelter. Don't forget:

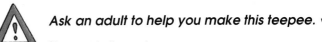

Pegs or safety pins hold it together.

A flashlight

Comics or a book

Extra blankets

A radio or walkman

Hot drink

Food rations

13

NORTH POLE TREK

In the Arctic it is always freezing cold and strong winds blow. Explorers have to travel across deep snow and ice on snowmobiles.

In this game, race the snowmobiles back to the igloos but watch out for the polar bears and the ice-holes!

You need:

Big sheet of white cardboard or posterboard ($15^1/_4$ in x $20^1/_2$ in)
Thick and thin colored paper
Felt-tip pens, straws
Poster-tack, glue
Craft knife, scissors, ruler

Igloos

Draw and cut out four igloos from thick paper. Give each one a number which will be its score. Bend along the dotted lines and glue the bases to the cardboard.

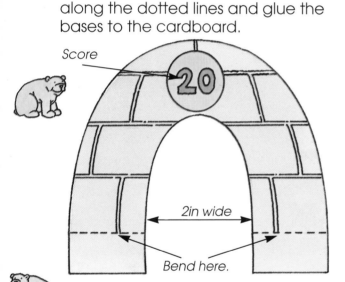

Score

2in wide

Bend here.

Polar bears

Draw and cut out five polar bears, with bases, from thick paper. Copy these or make up your own.

To make the bears stand up, bend along the dotted line.

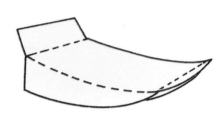

4in

1in

Snowmobiles

Copy this shape onto thin paper. Cut out three or four in different colors. Score and bend along the dotted lines to make them stand up.

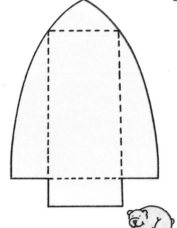

Board

Measure and draw lines 2in in from each side. Score and bend up slightly.

Glue the igloos along one end of the board.

Use a craft knife to cut out several ice holes.

Stick the polar bears on with poster-tack.

How to play

Prop up the board on books so that it slopes down towards the end with the igloos.

Each player in turn takes three tries at blowing the snowmobiles into the igloos. Use a straw and blow at the turned-up tail of the snowmobile. Score points for each one you get into an igloo. The number of points will depend on which igloo you enter.

If you fall through an ice hole or crash into a hungry polar bear, you lose your turn.

At the end of the game, the players add up their scores. The winner is the person who has scored the most points.

JUNGLE SAFARI

Jungles, or tropical rainforests, are hot, steamy places overgrown with trees, vines and other plants. They grow so thickly that explorers must use knives to cut their way through.

 Tropical rainforests grow close to the Equator, where it is very hot and damp. It rains nearly every day, often with thunder and lightning. After a downpour, it looks as if the jungle is steaming.

All kinds of amazing, colourful birds and animals live in the jungle. Here is an idea for a mural for your bedroom wall.

 You need:

Roll of plain wallpaper
  or lining paper
Colored paper
Felt-tip pens, paints
Cellophane tape
Poster-tack or glue
Scissors

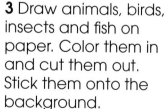 **1** Tape strips of wallpaper along the wall. Ask an adult's permission first!

2 Draw and color a background of trees, plants and flowers. Add a river in the foreground.

3 Draw animals, birds, insects and fish on paper. Color them in and cut them out. Stick them onto the background.

If you stick each creature on with poster-tack you can change around the scene whenever you like.

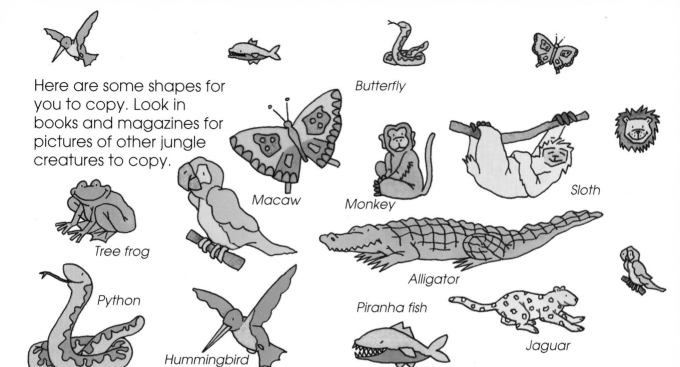

Here are some shapes for you to copy. Look in books and magazines for pictures of other jungle creatures to copy.

Butterfly

Macaw

Monkey

Sloth

Tree frog

Python

Hummingbird

Alligator

Piranha fish

Jaguar

The jungle is divided into levels from the treetops to the ground. Different plants and animals live at each level.

NATURE TRAIL

Many real explorers travelled through unknown lands, hoping to find new kinds of plants or animals. If you make this nature trail kit you can be a wildlife explorer too.

Explore the local park, woods, countryside, or your garden. Don't go exploring on your own. Take a group of friends or an adult with you.

Keep a record of what you see in a special notebook. Divide each page into four columns headed Date, Time, Place and Description.

Date	Place	Time	Description
Mon 7th	Garden	3.30pm	Green caterpillar
Tue 8th	Apple tree	4.00pm	Blue
Fri 10th	Front lawn	8.30 am	
Sat 11th	By the compost	10.00 am	Very hairy caterpillar
Sun 12th	Park	11.30 am	Big blue

Date	Place	Time	Description

Cover your notebook with colored paper and either draw or cut out and glue on paper bird, animals, plants and insects.

Bug jar

Here is a fun way to pick up tiny insects to examine without harming them. Release them as soon as you have studied them. Do not leave the jar in the sun or the insects will die.

Draw around one end of each tube onto the lid. Cut out the circles to make holes for the tubes. The tubes must fit tightly.

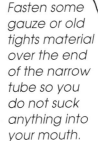

You need:

Small glass jar with plastic lid
$11^3/_4$in length plastic tubing x $^1/_4$in diameter
8in length plastic tubing x $^1/_4$in diameter
Craft knife
Pencil
Cotton balls
Gauze

Don't suck up insects that are too big as they might get damaged in the tube.

Cotton wool for a soft landing

Fasten some gauze or old tights material over the end of the narrow tube so you do not suck anything into your mouth.

Elastic band

Gauze or piece of old tights

Place the thick tube over bug.

Suck in through the thin tube.

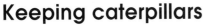

Keeping caterpillars

If you find a caterpillar, bring it home with some of the plant it was feeding on.

Keep it in a large jar or glass tank. It must be in a container big enough for its wings to spread when it turns into a butterfly or moth.

Watch it turn into a chrysalis and then, two or three weeks later, into a moth or butterfly.

Don't keep your moth a prisoner - let it go when it is strong enough to fly.

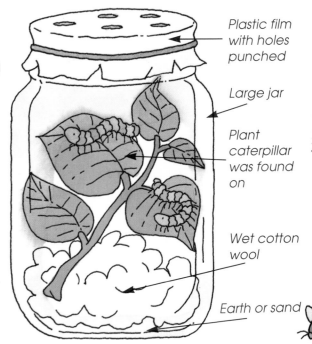

Plastic film with holes punched

Large jar

Plant caterpillar was found on

Wet cotton wool

Earth or sand

UNDERSEA ADVENTURE

Under the sea there is an amazing world to explore. It is full of strange and colorful wildlife, dramatic landscapes and exciting finds, such as sunken treasure.

Some undersea explorers dive with air tanks called aqualungs attached to them. With these they can explore the shallower ocean waters. Deep-sea explorers travel down thousands of meters in small submarines called submersibles.

Diving experiment

Here is a diving experiment to try.

You need:

Empty plastic bottle (1.5 liter)
Plastic from a food carton
Pen top
Rubber band
Plasticine or poster-tack

Make sure you draw the diver narrow enough to fit through the bottle neck

1 Draw a diver onto the plastic using a pencil. Cut it out. Decorate using waterproof paints.

Don't use a pen top with a hole here!

2 Stick a small lump of poster-tack or plasticine around the pen top without blocking the open end.

Don't cover the opening.

A slim, pointed pen top is best.

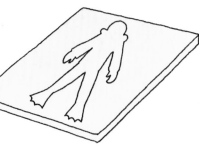

3 Fix the pen top to the diver with the rubber band.

20

4 Fill the bottle almost full with water. Put in the diver - it should just float.

5 Screw on the bottle cap. Squeeze the bottle and the diver will sink to the bottom. Let go and he or she will rise to the top.

You could decorate the bottle by sticking paper shapes of fish, seaweed, coral, even a sunken ship, around the outside with glue or double-sided tape.

If the diver is too light, or sinks, empty the bottle, take the diver out and adjust the amount of Plasticine. You may have to do this a few times to get it right.

Wrap plastic film around to keep them in place.

Diving language

In the water, real divers "talk" to one another in sign language like this:

Going up

Going down

Stop

Help!

OK

Something wrong

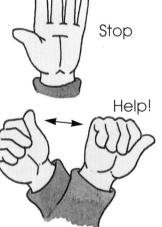

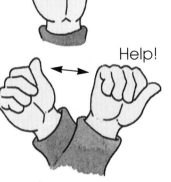

LOST TREASURE

Many explorers dream of being the first to discover a long-lost ancient city, or finding treasure that has stayed hidden for thousands of years.

Expeditions into unknown places can be difficult and dangerous. These explorers have found their way into a hidden chamber inside a pyramid. But the entrance is closing behind them! Can you help them find another way out?

SPACE JOURNEY

In space, there is no air to breathe and no gravity to stop astronauts floating away. Outside their space capsules, they must wear thick spacesuits for protection and carry oxygen tanks so that they can breathe.

A shellsuit or baggy tracksuit makes a great spacesuit.

Make a laser gun from an empty plastic bottle that has a handle. Decorate with foil and colored paper.

Wear old trainers or Wellington boots sprayed silver.

Oxygen pack

You need:

Large piece of cardboard or posterboard
2 empty plastic bottles
Plastic tubing
Colored paper
String, cellophane tape

Thread through string, long enough to cross over at the front and tie behind your back

Place one end of the plastic tubing through a hole in the side of the helmet.

Make holes at the top.

Place the other end of the plastic tubing in a bottle top and secure with tape.

Tape or glue the plastic bottles to the cardboard.

Paint or cover cardboard with aluminum foil or paper.

Helmet

You need:

Cardboard box big enough to fit over
  your head
Scissors or craft knife
Aluminum foil
Colored paper
Glue
String

1 Open out all the box flaps. Cut away the shaded areas at the front and back of the box.

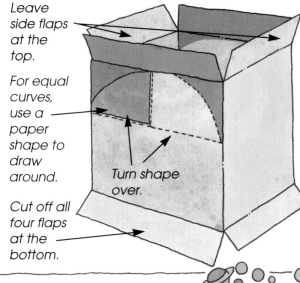

Leave side flaps at the top.

For equal curves, use a paper shape to draw around.

Turn shape over.

Cut off all four flaps at the bottom.

2 Cut out a square at the front for your face. Bend over side flaps and glue to curves.

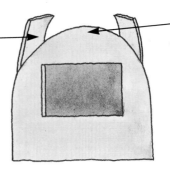

Curve over and glue.

Cover gap with foil.

3 Cut out a curved shape at each side so that the helmet fits over your shoulders. Make holes back and front, thread string through and tie under arms.

Paint or cover the helmet with foil or colored paper. Glue on cut-out or sticky stars and other shapes for decoration.

Alien masks

Space scientists say there could be other life in the universe. What do you think the "aliens" might look like? Here are some alien masks to make. Attach string to the sides to tie around your head.

Holes for eyes and mouth.

Thin cardboard

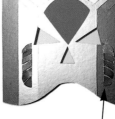

Antennae made from pipe cleaners and pieces of cork

Colored paper shapes glued on

Famous explorers

The **Vikings** from Scandinavia began exploring new territory as early as the 9th century, settling in Iceland and Greenland. It is now thought that Vikings in their longships were the first Europeans to discover America.

David Livingstone was the first European to walk right across Africa. He went missing in 1868 while searching for the source of the River Nile. Three years later he was found by Henry Stanley, an American who set out with an expedition to find him.

In the past, it was unusual for women to become explorers. **Mary Kingsley** began to travel in 1893. On her travels through Africa she faced many dangers and collected rare specimens of fish and insects.

Jacques Cousteau is a famous modern underwater explorer. He designed and experimented with new diving equipment and was the first to use underwater photography to learn more about sea-life.

In 1492, **Christopher Columbus** set sail from Spain for the Far East. He wanted to prove that the world was round not flat, so he sailed west instead of east. After two months, land was sighted. Columbus thought he had reached China, but he had in fact arrived at the Bahamas, off the coast of America. He returned to Spain a hero, and died without ever knowing the importance of his discovery.

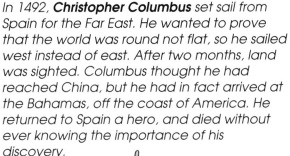

Meriwether Lewis and **William Clark** were the first Europeans to explore America from the Mississippi River to the west coast. It took them over two years, from 1804 to 1806, to travel 13,000 kilometers.

In 1911, a team of Norwegians, led by **Roald Amundsen**, became the first people to reach the South Pole. They just beat a British expedition led by **Captain Robert Scott**. Sadly, on the return journey, all five members of the British team died from the cold.

Mountain explorers, **Sir Edmund Hillary** and **Tenzing Norgay**, were the first men to reach the top of Mount Everest, the highest mountain in the world. They did this in 1952.

In 1961, Soviet cosmonaut **Yuri Gagarin** became the first person to travel into space. In 1969, US astronaut **Neil Armstrong** became the first person to walk on the moon.

Survival tips

In the desert

Carry as much water as possible. If you run out, conserve the water in your body by travelling at night when it is cooler. Some desert plants contain water that you can try to squeeze out.

In the tropics

Cover your body against mosquitoes and other insects. Shake out your shoes, clothes and bedding before use in case insects or snakes have crawled in!

In polar regions

Prevent frostbite by keeping warm, eating and drinking warm drinks.

In the water

Wear a lifejacket at all times. Keep your head out of water. Use air-filled clothes to help keep you afloat.

Signalling

The following are recognized as distress signals throughout the world.

Use stones and pieces of wood to write on the ground. Find a large clearing that can be spotted from the air.

Help!

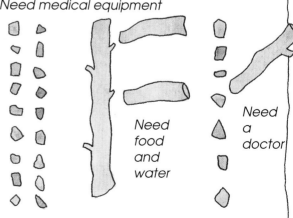

Need medical equipment

Need food and water

Need a doctor

EXPLORING WORDS

Aliens Beings from another planet.

Antarctic The frozen land surrounding the South Pole.

Aqualung Diving apparatus with air carried in containers on the diver's back.

Arctic The frozen land and sea around the North Pole.

Climate The type of weather in an area.

Equator The imaginary line around the middle of the Earth.

Expedition An organized journey to explore a place.

Gravity The force that keeps us on the ground.

Igloo Dome-shaped shelter built from blocks of snow.

Kit Supplies and equipment.

Navigate Find the way, usually following a map.

North Pole The point on the Earth that is furthest north.

Pitch camp Set up a shelter for the night.

Pyramid An ancient Egyptian monument.

Rations Share of food and water.

Route Planned path of a journey.

Safari A journey, especially in Africa.

Shelter Place to keep you dry, warm and comfortable, such as a tent, cave, or shelter built from natural materials.

Site Place to pitch camp.

SOS Distress signal.

South Pole The point on the Earth that is furthest south.

Specimen Object collected for study.

Submersible Small submarine.

Supplies Food, water and equipment.

Survive To stay alive.

Terrain Ground or landscape.

Territory An area of land.

Trail A route or path.

Trek A long journey.

Tropical Climate that is hot and rainy.

Index